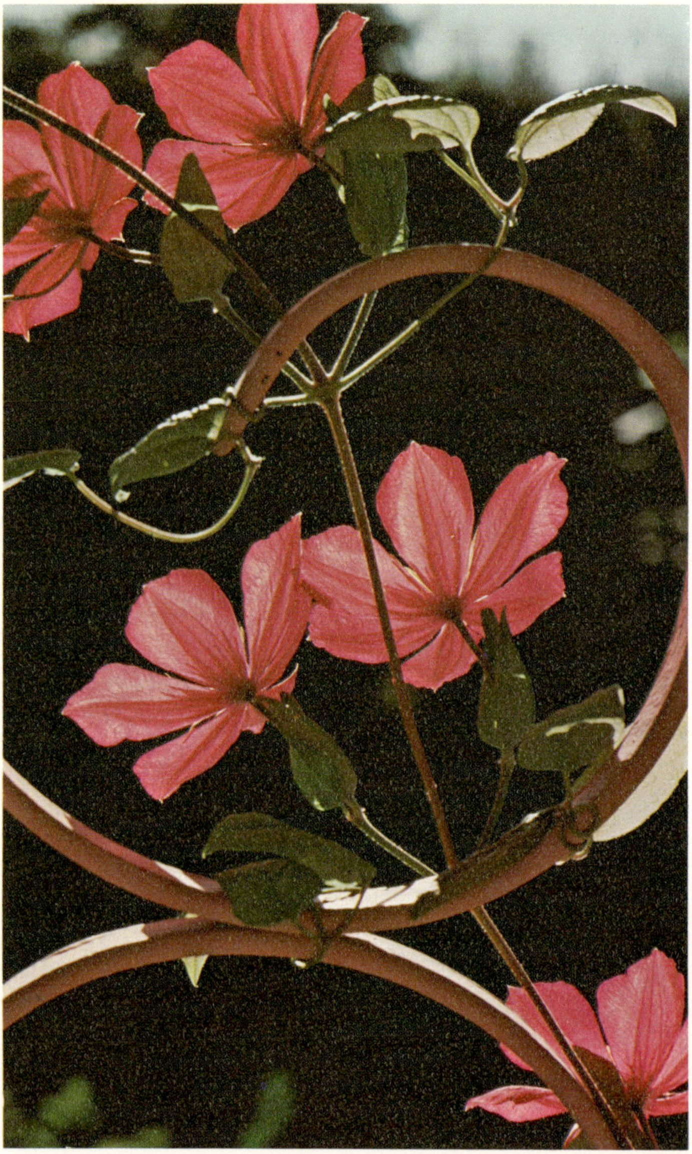

GREAT WORDS OF TODAY

THE BEST OF TWENTIETH CENTURY WIT AND WISDOM

The C.R. Gibson Company
Norwalk, Connecticut

Copyright © MCMLXXIX by
The C.R. Gibson Company
Norwalk, Connecticut
All rights reserved
Printed in the United States of America
(ISBN: 0-8378-5018-5)

Today's thoughts by "today" people... sometimes serious, sometimes humorous, but always fascinating—just like life today!

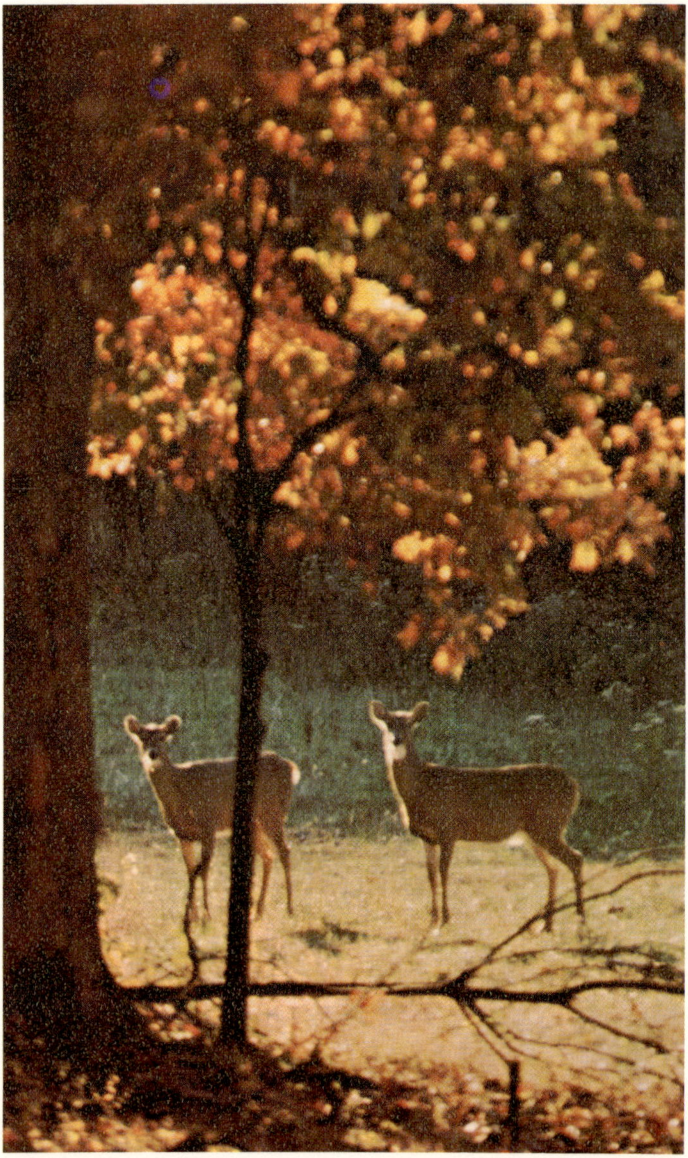

> Ninety per cent of life is just showing up.
>
> *Woody Allen*

Do it NOW. Time is money. Work smarter, not harder. There's always enough time for the important things.

Alan Lakein

> Change is the law of life. And those who look only to the past are certain to miss the future.
>
> *John F. Kennedy*

It's when you're safe at home that you wish you were having an adventure. When you're having an adventure you wish you were safe at home.

Thornton Wilder

> Experience is what makes you recognize a mistake when you make it again.
>
> *Earl Wilson*

Many creatures have brains, but only humans have in addition to their brains, phenomenal minds.

Buckminster Fuller

This I know. This I believe with all my heart. If we want a free and peaceful world, if we want to make deserts bloom and man grow to greater dignity as a human being—we can do it!

Eleanor Roosevelt

One of the best ways to relax that I know of is to pull weeds.

Robert Wilder

I loved to arrive in a new place and face the new situations, like one newly born who sees life for the first time, when it still has the air of fiction. It lasts one day.

Saul Steinberg

I want a *lot* of fun. I think fun is really important, as important as obeyin' the Golden Rule and abolishin' war and electin' the right candidates.
> Shirley MacLaine

Comedy is sympathy.
> Bert Lahr

All your fingernails grow with inconvenient speed except the broken one.
> Ogden Nash

Nothing is as fleeting as a moment of wit on television.
> David Steinberg

Basically, I work to please myself. But I'm the hardest person to please that I know.
> Vincente Minnelli

Love, inspiration and a zest for the challenges of life are not the kind of gifts that can be wrapped in sparkling paper and set beneath a tree. But if one receives these gifts, one can pass them on.

Ted Kennedy

Each of us is born with a natural feeling of elation and optimism which is lost by too many in growing up.

Samm Sinclair Baker

I rather love the world. It is fantastically exciting and diverse, infinitely threaded with gold.

Richard Burton

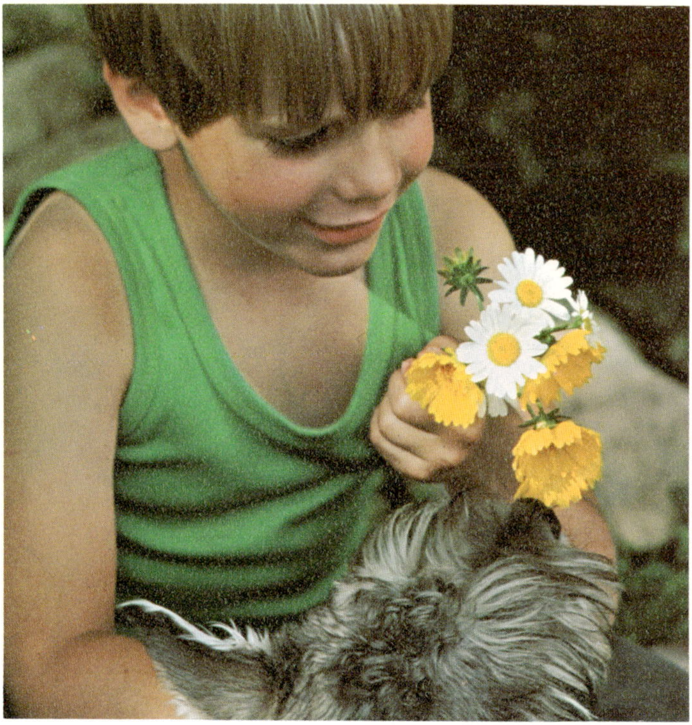

There is too much music without reason, without listening. Music in barber shops and manicure parlors and airports and elevators. It doesn't *arouse* anything. It is humdrum. Music should be *listened* to.

Arthur Fiedler

I never look back. I only look forward to what will be—where or when.

Richard Rogers

When people say it's silly for a grown man to earn his living playing games, I answer them this way: "If you can get paid for doing something you like, that's the greatest...I don't care what it is."

O.J. Simpson

This was my school—the movies.

Mel Brooks

Sooner or later every scientific enterprise comes to a fork in the road.
Dr. Thomas Szasz

The life of the creative man is led, directed and controlled by boredom. Avoiding boredom is one of our most important purposes. It is also one of the most difficult, because the amusement always has to be newer and on a higher level.
Saul Steinberg

The most incomprehensible thing about the world is that it is comprehensible.
Albert Einstein

I remain just one thing, and one thing only — and that is a clown. It places me on a far higher plane than any politician.
Charles Chaplin

...Only in quietness can I hear the tides of my own thoughts. Only in darkness can I discover the stars.
Alex Noble

One is not born a woman, one becomes one.
Simone de Beauvoir

The deepest thoughts are those that are left unsaid.

                    S.J. Perelman

Anything I learned that was truly important was learned out of school. I'm talking about human nature.

                    Robert Redford

Yesterday, staying at home to raise a family was a woman's destiny; today it is her choice. Tomorrow, every woman at home will have strong reasons for her decision.

Arlene Cardozo

When we know what we truly are, as women, you'll be able to be truly yourselves, as men.

Betty Friedan

Unlike a lot of couples, Joanne and I don't have a great deal in common beside our family and acting. We are very lucky.

Paul Newman

Hate and love, after all, are nearly one; a blow can be a kiss out of heaven, and a kiss a blow out of hell.

Dylan Thomas

There are too many men in politics and not enough elsewhere.

Hermione Gingold

When everybody is equal men will be able to cry and ask directions at a gas station and do all kinds of neat things.

Cher

It is important to know as much as possible about the workings of someone you love.

Audrey Hepburn

Being a Greek, I lean toward the dark side of the moon. I'm where the tears are. All I can do is cry when I see that so much romance has gone out of the world...

Telly Savalas

I think the older you get, the more you are struck with that "brightness" God gives, the more you find light alone to be a wonderful thing...

Rosalind Russell

Life is a mystery, all right, but not one we can solve with the right set of clues; nor is it a puzzle with one correct fit.

Gail Sheehy

Children are for loving—loving what they remind us of about ourselves, loving their being most human, loving the possibilities they bring, loving the miracle of life.

Eda LeShan

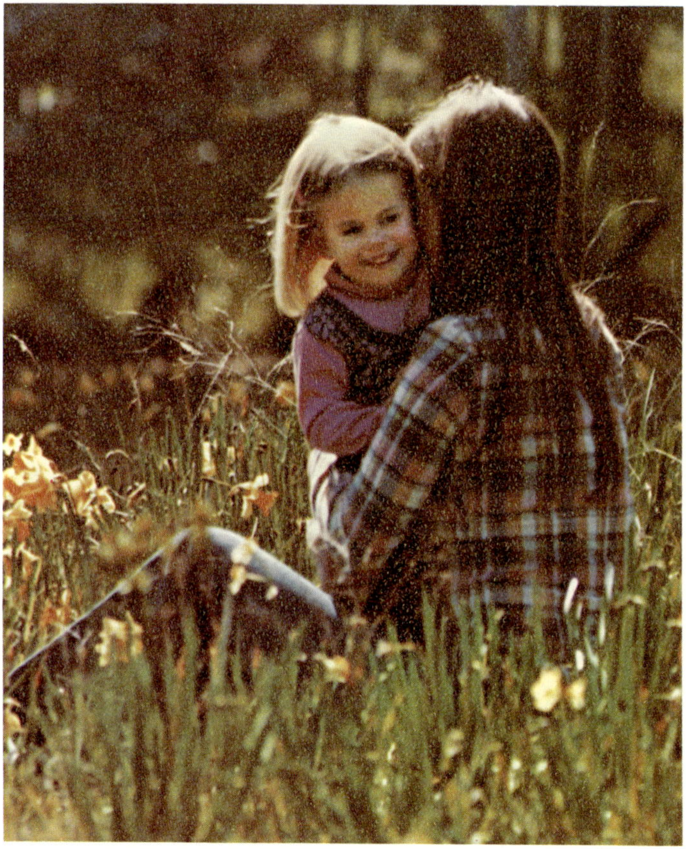

I've got about a thousand new things I'd like to try.

                                                  Willie Nelson

Everybody thinks of changing humanity and nobody thinks of changing himself.

                                                  Leo Tolstoy

We stand today in danger of forgetting the use of our hands. To forget how to dig the earth and tend the soil is to forget ourselves.

                                                  Mohandas K. Gandhi

Eat half as much, sleep twice as much, drink three times as much, laugh four times as much, and you will live to a ripe old age.

                                                  John Harvey Kellogg

I'm a duty man, a workaholic.

                                                  Hubert Humphrey

Many of us have the unrealistic belief that having to live with problems day after day is an unhealthy or unnatural lifestyle. Not so! Life presents us all with problems. It is entirely natural.

Dr. Manuel Smith

Ask not for whom the telephone bell tolls; if thou art in the tub, it tolls for thee.

James Thom

The fellow who says he's too old to learn new tricks probably always was.

A.J. Marshall

Don't look back. Somethin' might be gaining on you.

Satchel Paige

Thinking is the hardest work there is, which is the probable reason why so few engage in it.

Henry Ford

My idea of how to handle criticism is to go hide in the closet.
Helen Gurley Brown

Life is absolutely super and wonderful. There shouldn't be any sadness in it. People should be aware of all things at all times, they should experience the extremities of life, fulfill themselves completely. Why does everyone want to go to sleep when the only thing left is to stay awake?
Edward Albee

It is not easy to find happiness in ourselves, and it is not possible to find it elsewhere.

Agnes Repplier

The worst kind of loneliness is when you're right there with other people and you still feel lonely—because you're different, somehow.

Marlo Thomas

I don't want to achieve immortality through my work. I want to achieve it through not dying.

Woody Allen

Never look down to test the ground before taking your step: only he who keeps his eye fixed on the far horizon will find his right road.

Dag Hammarskjöld

Punishment must be intelligent and quick. Never hit your child unless it be in self-defense.

Sam Levenson

The most difficult thing in the world is to know how to do a thing and to watch somebody else doing it wrong, without comment.

T.G. White

If there's one thing I hate more than not being taken seriously, it's being taken too seriously.

Billy Wilder

Only when you learn to laugh at mankind's imperfections can you laugh at your own.
Dr. Joyce Brothers

Even with perfect recognition of the fact that we cannot be liked by everyone, we are always shocked to discover that someone does not like us.
Olgivanna Lloyd Wright

People shouldn't have goals except to be happy. If you have specific goals and then accomplish them, you die mentally.
Ernest Tidyman

Self-respect comes when you can stand on your own two feet. When you are able to take responsibility for yourself, when you are able to verify yourself.
Henry Winkler

Happiness is the art of making a bouquet of those flowers within reach.
Bob Goddard

The object of living is to have something left over after the nitty-gritty for other interests.
Anne Morrow Lindbergh

Find your style, your rhythm in life, your creative talents. As you accept and then develop your special individuality, you'll be energized, positive and enthusiastic. Finding *you* will send you soaring with vibrant joy.
Marabel Morgan

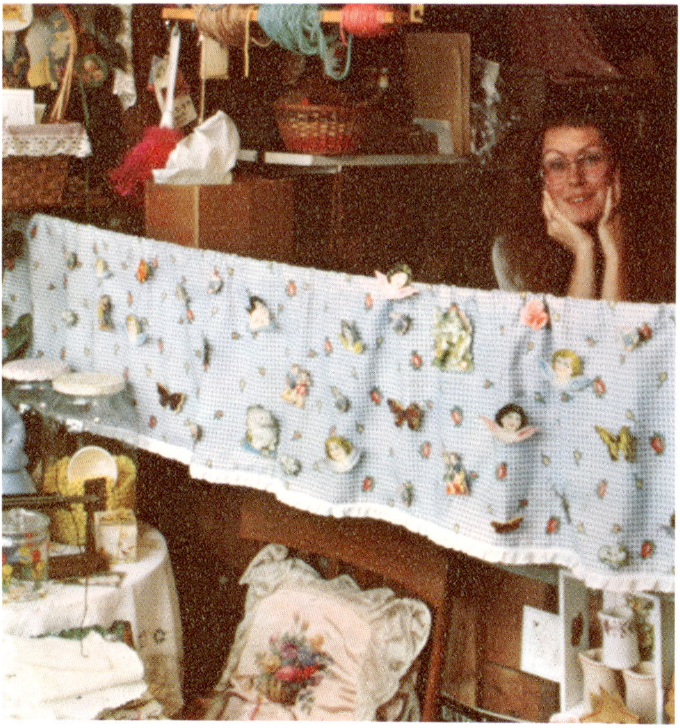

I am...sometimes out of control. But when there is real trouble, the nervousness gets pushed down so far that calm takes its place, and although I pay high for disaster when it is long past, I am not sure that real trouble registers on me when it first appears.

Lillian Hellman

...as long as you are affected by the way other people look on you, you are not free to enjoy what you have and do; you are letting the people around you infect you...

Liv Ullmann

Life is an interlocking jigsaw puzzle.

Theodore Reik

Whatever the grubbiness of our lot as earthlings may be, we know that there is some of the sky in us.

Hilton Gregory

...Everyone has his own reality. There is no one truth; everyone has their own, and the art of living is to know your own reality and respect that of others.

Barbra Streisand

In all of us there is a desire, marrow-deep, to know our heritage—to know who we are and where we have come from.

Alex Haley

"Well, hello there, little girl. And what do you want to be when you grow up?" I used to retort: "An adult." But secretly, I longed to be Brenda Starr.

Carol Burnett

If you live and grow, your commitment is to life, and love comes in that same spirit—love that is a joyous desire to share all that is best in yourself and others.

Stanton Peele

What is the most precious, the most exciting smell waiting for you in the house when you return to it after half-a-dozen years or so? The smell of roses, you think? No, mouldering books.
Andrel Sinyavsky

I may not be much good on day-to-day things, but I always rise to the occasion. It must be the ham in me.
Betty Ford

Plant a flower in a pot and its growth is limited to the size of the container. But plant it in a field and something different happens. Open to the sunlight and air, with space to expand, it can grow to the extent of its capacity for growth.
Nena O'Neill and George O'Neill

Anyone can be an artist at being *alive*.
Victor Candell

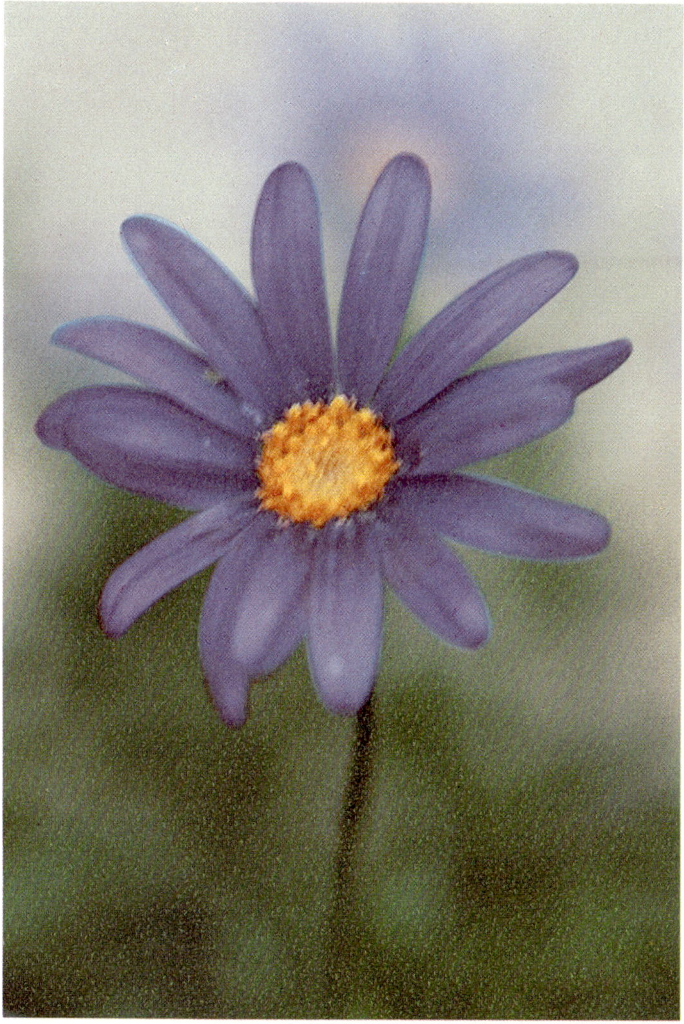

It is getting harder to compliment women. They're tired of empty words, of being compared to flowers, landscapes, climates and other irrelevancies. They've changed, and the descriptions of them will have to change.
Anatole Broyard

In work, love and the movies, everything is a fight.
Lina Wertmuller

To me, women's liberation means that every woman ought to be able to pursue whatever career or personal lifestyle she chooses as a full and equal member of society without fear of sexual discrimination.
Billie Jean King

I never hated a man enough to give him diamonds back.
Zsa Zsa Gabor

There *is* hope in the very presence of others, in their concern, even if they are completely powerless to change those things we must face, those events we call fate.

Gerald Moore

No novice has ever accomplished anything of importance. Two exceptions may be made. The Asbury Park Baby Parade and the Atlantic City Beauty Contest.

Amelia Earhart

...Horizons are never lost. I must search the infinite reaches of hope to discover where...and why.

Godfrey John

People have to acquire a good deal of skill in character reading if they are to live a single year of life without disaster.

Virginia Woolf

Qualities I look for in a friend? Well, what I find irresistible is enthusiasm.

Katharine Hepburn

All my life I have had a great, roaring faith in this country.

Lady Bird Johnson

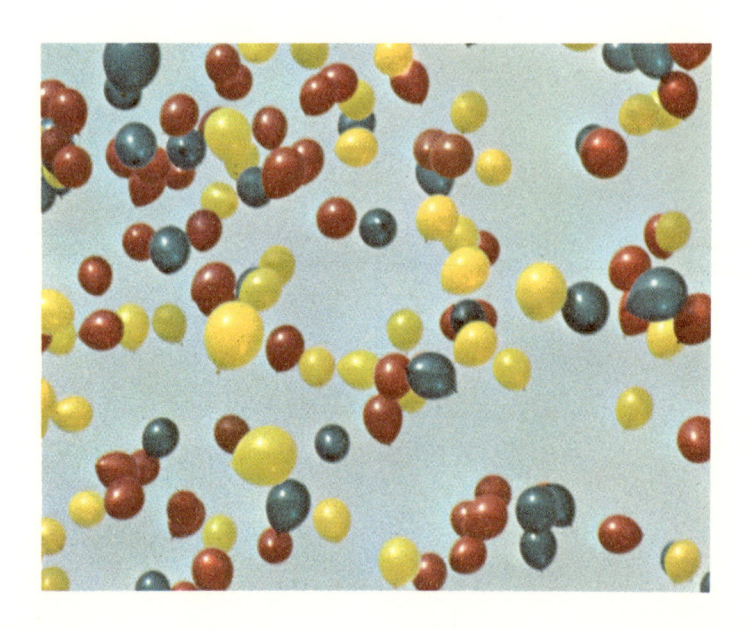

American society is still not perfect, but it is still the best there is.

Gerald Ford

What a gamble friendship is!

E.B. White

In my experience, the only thing you can quit cold turkey is cold turkey.

Jean Kerr

America is a nation of incessant change, and I have always believed that such a condition was good for people of energy and imagination.

James Michener

Personally I'm always ready to learn, although I do not always like being taught.

Winston Churchill

America means opportunity. It started that way.

Neil A. Armstrong

Never discuss a new idea with people at lunch, dinner, breakfast or in bed. They will eat it or get up with it.

Jane Trahey

If you want to develop individuality, you should be able to work harmoniously with all kinds of people.
Paul Tillich

The Presidency is an all-day and nearly an all-night job. Just between you and me and the gatepost, I like it.
Harry S. Truman

Americans have more timesaving devices and less time than any other group of people in the world.
Duncan Caldwell

Look with suspicion upon such slogans as "You can't argue with success." You can, and should.
Sam Levenson

The very best way to strengthen love is through *acts* of love. An act of love is one with no other purpose—a pure expression of feeling that is not disguised in any way.

Dr. George Weinberg

Motherhood is a gift. I don't think it's a talent or anything frightfully out of the ordinary.

Nancy Walker

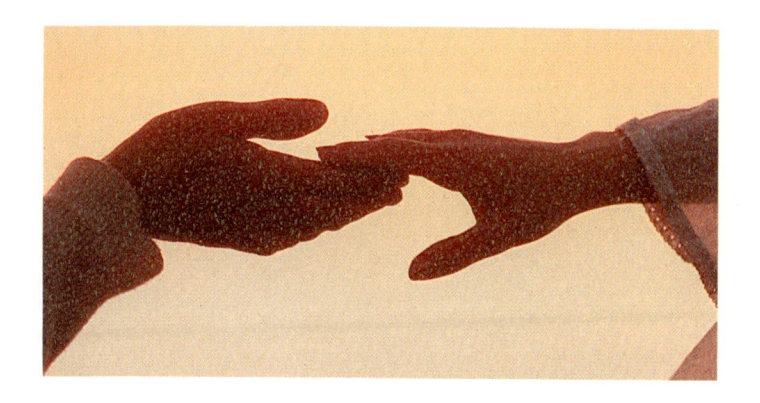

There are three ways to get something done: do it yourself, hire someone or forbid your kids to do it.

Monta Crane

Sometimes when I think I'd like to be single again—I think again.

Judith Viorst

I don't know any parents who have total communication with their children. *I* don't have, and I didn't with *my* parents. There has to be the moment of rebellion.

Joanne Woodward

The workings of the mind and of the *soul* are about as little understood today as the workings of the heart were sixty years ago.

      Dr. Paul Dudley White

I've found that if you can just last through the rough spots, and hold onto the good spots, things will always get better. They always have.

      Lillian Carter

They say you can't do it but that doesn't always work.

      Casey Stengal

To be a good winner, you gotta know how to be a loser. If you win right off the bat, it doesn't mean anything.

      Johnny Paycheck

...the evidence points to the conclusion that it is *natural* to be happy, loving and full of joy.

Dr. Wayne W. Dyer

The most luxurious possession, the richest treasure anybody has, is his personal dignity.

Jackie Robinson

I never liked the middle ground — the most boring place in the world.

Louise Nevelson

Nobody likes a sad bartender.

Art Buchwald

The full enjoyment of life is the best prescription for staying healthy.

Dr. Art Ulene

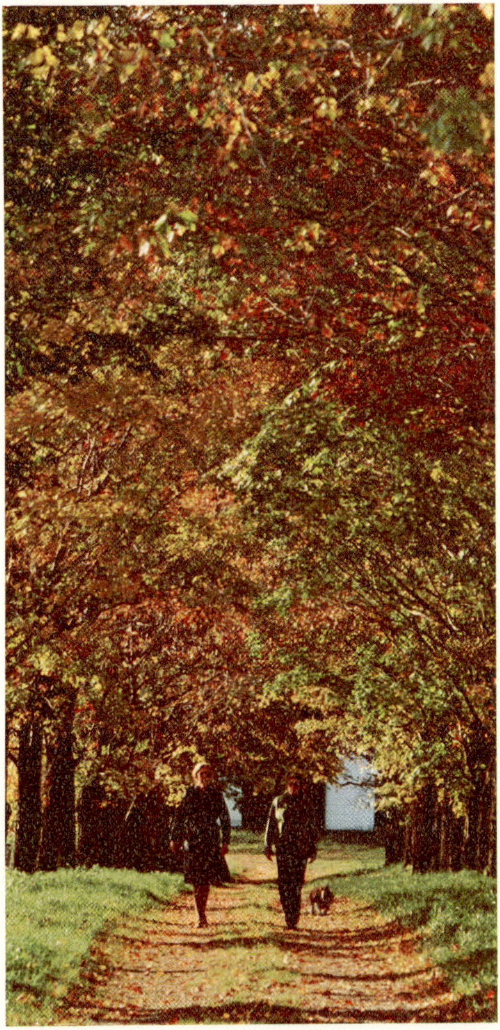

Everyone wants to understand art. Why not try to understand the song of a bird? Why does one love the night, flowers, everything around one, without trying to understand them?

Pablo Picasso

Poetry is the achievement of the synthesis of hyacinths and biscuits.

Carl Sandburg

You only live once, and by acting you can live a million lives.

Diane Nabatoff

I believe in the immortality of the theater. It is the happiest loophole of escape for those who have secretly put their childhood in their pockets and have gone off with it to play to the end of their days.

Edward G. Robinson

Life only demands from you the strength you possess. Only one feat is possible—not to have run away.

Dag Hammarskjöld

Reading is a joy, but not an unalloyed joy. Books do not make life easier or more simple, but harder and more interesting.

Harry Golden

Parents want their children to have only the best. They feed them Brie cheese, when the kids would prefer Hostess cupcakes.

Joel Fram

I think . . . we are living in a time of journalism where you go out of your way to find things wrong; you look for the seams instead of the material.

Barbara Walters

...Birds and grass and generations of people go on endlessly.

Gerald Moore

I am so tired of smiling, always looking pretty and behaving well. I'm just getting tired of being a lady.

Candice Bergen

It is a mistake to believe that the contemporary wars and depressions and political threats are the total cause of our anxiety, for our anxiety also causes these catastrophes.

Rollo May

An idea is probably the most vulnerable property a creative person owns.

Jane Trahey

Do I ever lie? Oh, yes. I couldn't live without it.

Lillian Carter

Love is like quicksilver in the hand. Leave the fingers open and it stays in the palm; clutch it and it darts away.

Dorothy Parker

Once, just once before I die, I'd like
to see my hipbones.

Erma Bombeck

Why does a woman work ten years to change a
man's habits and then complain that he's not the
man she married?

Barbra Streisand

When one exercises his inalienable right to line a bureau drawer with newspaper on a humid day and deposit in it a couple of freshly ironed shirts, it's a cinch the resultant decalcomania on his bosom will eventually elicit comment from some busybody or other.

S.J. Perelman

No learner has ever run short of subjects to explore.

Gilbert Highet

One of the secrets of a long and fruitful life is to forgive everybody everything before you go to bed at night.

Bernard Baruch

A radical is a man with both feet firmly planted in the air.

Franklin D. Roosevelt

...Pinpricks sometimes irritate more than deep wounds.
  Bruce Gould

I really believe that it is a wonderful idea to find out what your guy wants and then help him get it. That's being a real woman.
  Karen Black

In my world there are realities that always remain constant: to decrease suffering and increase joy.
  Dr. Alice Ginott

The man who wants to put on the brakes instead of stepping on the gas usually has fewer ideas about where to go.
  Webster Schott

I would say, categorically, that single women are often more interesting than married ones...I always *did* say that. Singles *try* harder.

Helen Gurley Brown

Many lonely, unloved people assume that finding the right person is what they need in order to love. Love is up to you, *not them*.

Bob Hoffman

Turn your thoughts to being a happy, confident, effective human being, and stop worrying about having to have something, and it usually ends up right in your lap.

Dr. Wayne W. Dyer

To appreciate fully any countryside, you have to live with it through all the changes in the seasons.

Elinore Graham

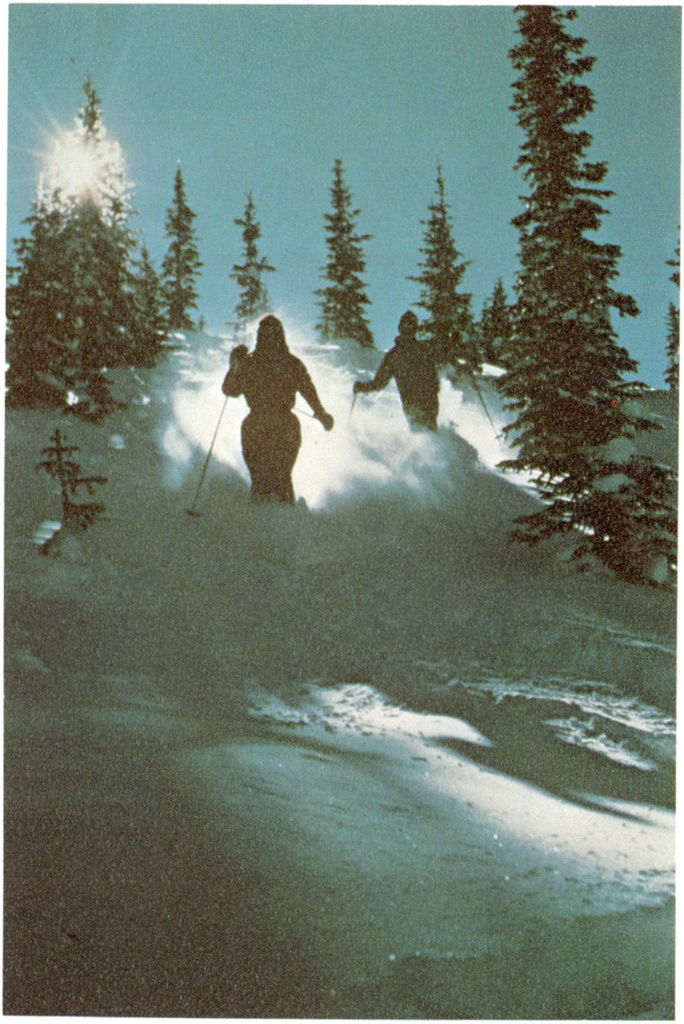

The golden rule of friendship is to listen to others as you would have them listen to you.

David Augsburger

We, the people, are the boss, and we will get the kind of political leadership, be it good or bad, that we demand and deserve.

John F. Kennedy

I was too heavy to be a jockey and unfit for honest work, so I became a writer.

Leon Uris

If I ever have to ask someone to work on New Year's Eve, I want them to be sure that I have already done 17 times more work on the project than I am asking them to do.

Ralph Nader

Joy is having a reason for living. Joy is having belief. Joy is knowing that you are part of an historical force that can make life better for people.
Jane Fonda

Taking charge of your life cannot be done for you. It is a right that only you can take for yourself.
Mildred Newman and Bernard Berkowitz

We are history, but without art's recording and preserving of history, it might as well have never existed.
Catharine Morris Wright

Nice guys finish last.
Leo Durocher

Traveling is like falling in love; the world is made new.
          Jan Myrdal and Gun Kessle

I don't think you can be truly funny unless there has been some suffering.
          Carol Burnett

God must love housewives as He does the poor. He makes so many of us.
          Phyllis McGinley

Nothing lives on so fresh and evergreen as the love with a funnybone.
          George Jean Nathan

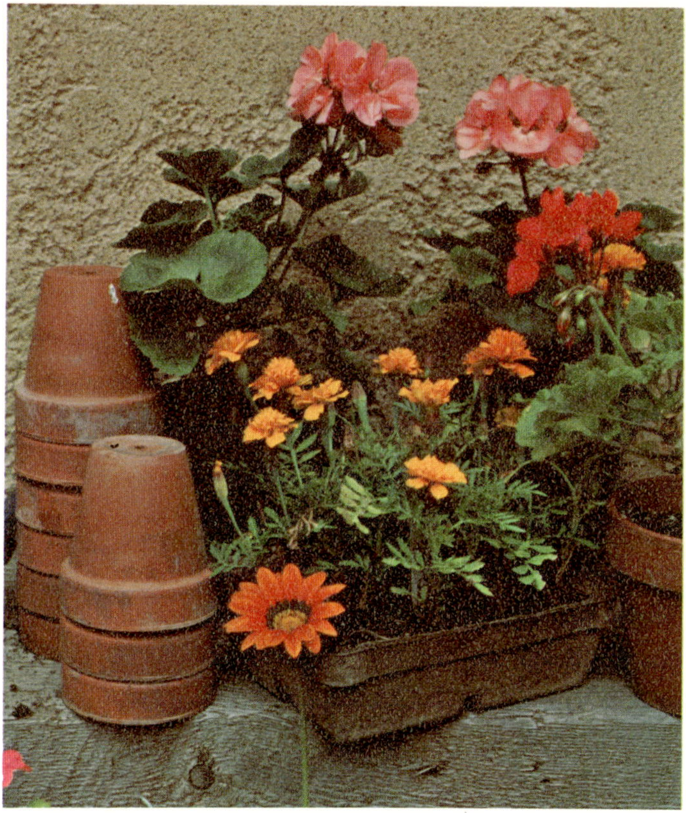

Selected by Barbara Shook Hazen
Designed by Sandra Kopell,
Publishers Graphics
Type set in Optima

Photo Credits:
Gene Ruestmann, cover, p. 38; John Taylor, p. 2; Robert F. Lee, p. 6; Jay Johnson, pp. 11, 55; Jeff Munk, p. 14; Marie Demarest, pp. 15, 39; Pat Powers, p. 19; Alan Blank, pp. 22-23; Jim Patrick, pp. 27, 42, 46-47; Beth Welsh, p. 31; Bob Kolbrener, p. 34; Four By Five, Inc., p. 35; Janet Nelson, p. 51.